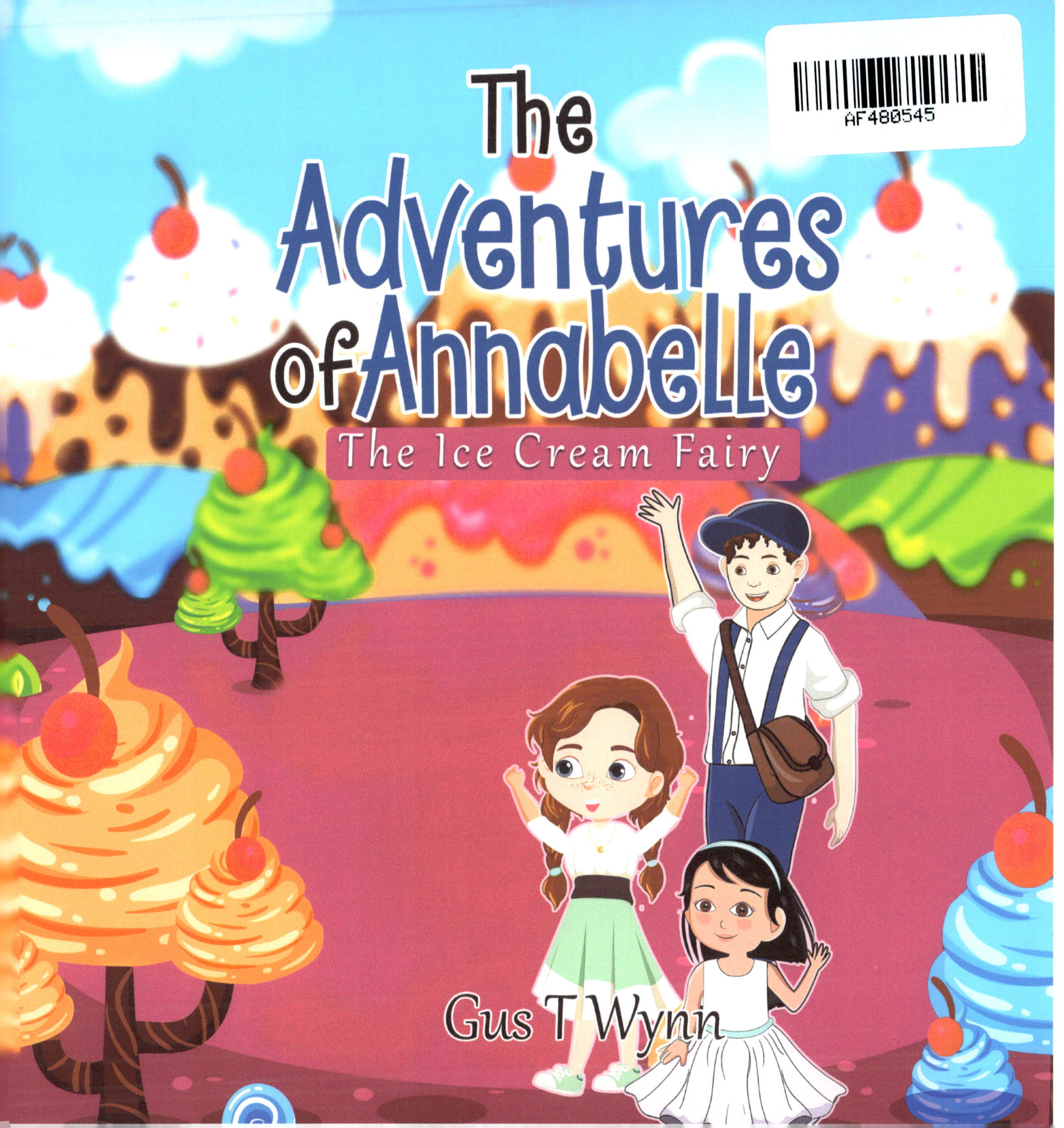

AF480545
The
Adventures
of Annabelle
The Ice Cream Fairy
Gus T Wynn

DEDICATION

To my son, Oliver, Peach, Lola Daisy, my dear departed parents, Al and Yetta; and to my amazing family. To all the children and parents that have been through Saint Jude Children's Cancer Research Hospital. In addition, I would like to say that each and every penny generated by this book is donated to Saint Jude Children's Cancer Research Hospital.

ACKNOWLEDGMENT

Many thanks to B.L. Watson, who is a major contributor to this project, and, of course, the fine people at Barnes Ghost Writing, who held my hand throughout this entire process. And of course, the illustrators who brought Annabelle and the story to life. Lastly, I would like to thank all the doctors, nurses, and staff at Saint Jude's Children's Research Hospital for giving me the motivation and inspiration to create the story.

ABOUT THE AUTHOR

My name is Gus T. Wynn. I have had the most incredible life with amazing parents and wonderful sisters. My hobbies are so diverse that it would take another book to list them all. These include raising exotic animals, extensive world travel, cheffing, fishing, farming, underwater photography, and, of course, writing children's books, just to name a few. I am a true hobbyist at heart and never stop learning.

CHAPTER 1

Once upon a time, there was a curious little girl named Annabelle who loved to explore. She lived in a cozy village filled with friendly people, cute animals, and lots of yummy treats.

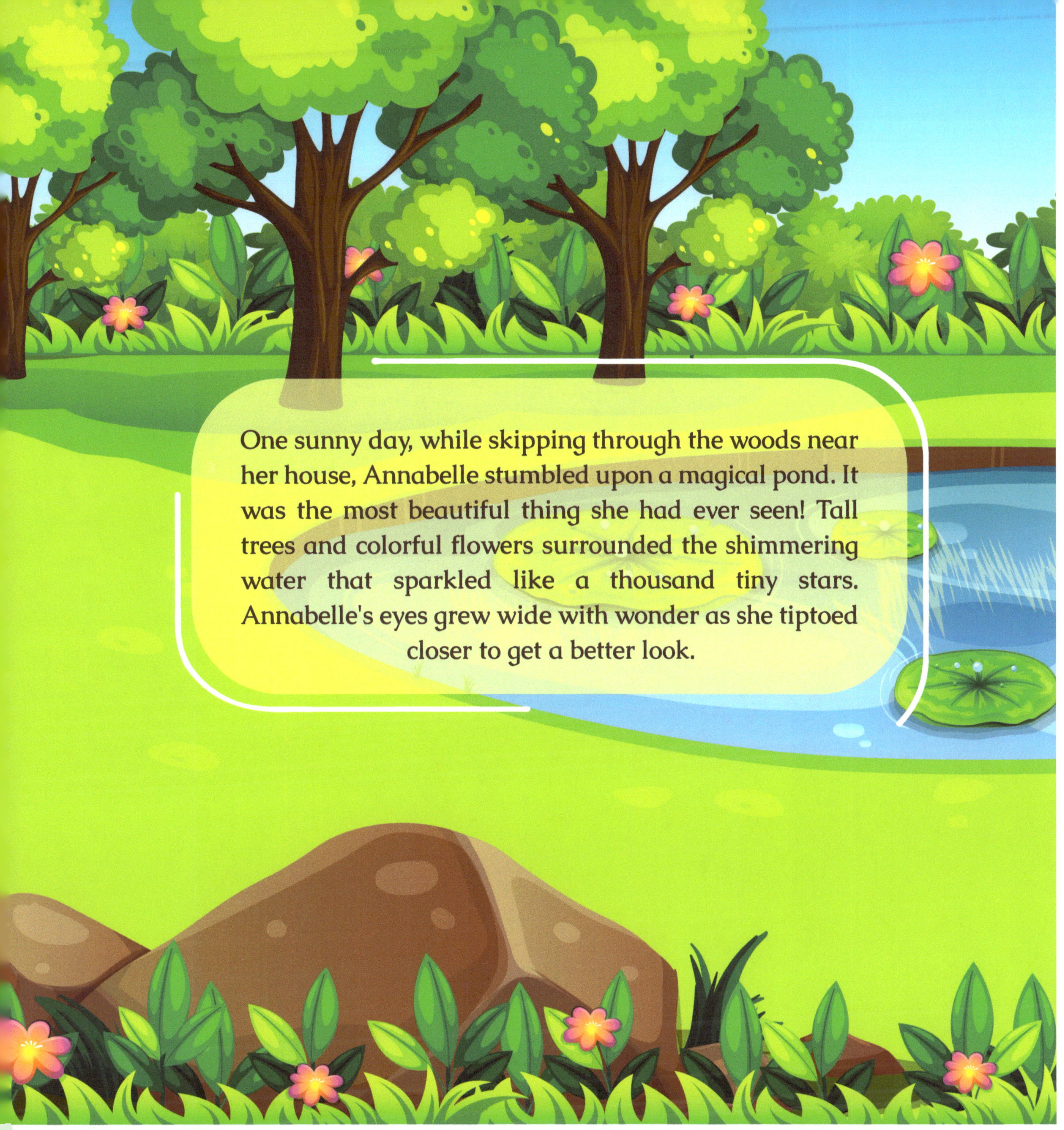One sunny day, while skipping through the woods near her house, Annabelle stumbled upon a magical pond. It was the most beautiful thing she had ever seen! Tall trees and colorful flowers surrounded the shimmering water that sparkled like a thousand tiny stars. Annabelle's eyes grew wide with wonder as she tiptoed closer to get a better look.

As she approached the edge of the pond, the water started to swirl and dance, like something amazing was about to happen. Annabelle watched in awe as a big, fluffy cow emerged from the whirling water. The cow had a coat of white and brown patches, a friendly smile, and a voice that boomed like thunder.

"Well hello there, Annabelle!" the cow said cheerfully. "I am the magical cow of this enchanted pond. I have the power to grant you one special wish. What would you like most in the whole wide world?"

Annabelle couldn't believe her luck! Meeting a real magical creature was a dream come true. After thinking it over for a moment, she exclaimed, "I wish I could make yummy ice cream for everyone, all the time!"

With a twinkle in its eye, the magical cow smiled and nodded. And just like that, Annabelle's wish was granted! A huge, colorful mountain of ice cream appeared before her very eyes. There were scoops of chocolate, vanilla, and strawberry, some with sprinkles, some with gooey syrup, and some with crunchy waffle cones. It was the most mouthwatering sight Annabelle had ever laid eyes on.

After thanking her new magical friend, Annabelle raced home with the biggest grin to share the exciting news (and the delicious ice cream) with her family. From that day forward, Annabelle became known far and wide as the ice cream fairy. With her amazing new powers, she could whip up any flavor, any topping, any time! All the children and grown-ups in the village would come to Annabelle for a sweet, creamy treat to brighten their day.

Annabelle had many more adventures, using her ice cream magic to spread joy wherever she went. She learned that the greatest happiness comes from sharing what you have and being kind to others. And though she could have kept the ice cream all to herself, Annabelle knew in her heart that treats taste best when you have friends to share them with.

As time passed, whenever Annabelle visited the special pond in the woods, she would think back on that fateful day she met the magical talking cow. Little did she know then what an incredible journey she was about to begin as the one and only ice cream fairy!

CHAPTER 2

Word of Annabelle's ice cream magic spread like wildfire and soon people were coming from villages far and wide to get a taste. One day, a little boy named Tommy heard about the amazing ice cream fairy. Tommy had never tried ice cream before and the thought of it made his mouth water. With an excited spring in his step, Tommy set off on the path to Annabelle's village.

Tommy skipped past green, grassy fields speckled with flowers and splashed through babbling brooks. As he got closer, a sweet, inviting smell tickled his nose – it was vanilla! Tommy heard the sound of children laughing and the clinking of ice cream cones. He knew he must be close.

When Tommy finally reached Annabelle, he saw her building a tall, teetering tower out of pointy ice cream cones in every color of the rainbow. Shyly, Tommy approached her and said, "Hi Annabelle, I'm Tommy. I've come from far away because I heard you make the best ice cream in the whole world. May I pretty please try some?"

Annabelle turned to Tommy with a warm, friendly smile. "Of course you can, Tommy! I would love to share some ice cream with you." She plopped a humongous scoop of bright pink strawberry on a cone for him. It was piled so high it looked like a puffy cotton candy cloud!

Tommy gave the ice cream a lick and his eyes lit up with glee. The sweet, fruity flavor danced on his tongue and made his taste buds sing. He couldn't help but giggle as he savored every bite. "Annabelle, this is incredible! I've never tasted anything so yummy in my whole life!"

Annabelle chuckled, happy to see Tommy so delighted. "I'm thrilled you like it, Tommy. I've learned that ice cream has a special way of making people smile."

As Tommy gobbled up the last bites, a question popped into his mind. "Annabelle, what's the secret to making your ice cream so magical?"

Annabelle leaned in with a twinkle in her eye and said, "Well Tommy, it's not just the fresh cream, sweet flavors, and fun toppings I use. The real magic is the joy and love I pour into each and every scoop. When you make ice cream with a happy heart and share it with friends, it tastes even more wonderful."

Tommy nodded, understanding completely. His young mind could sense the deeper wisdom behind her words. With a grateful smile, he said, "Thank you so much Annabelle, for the ice cream and for teaching me about real magic. This has been the greatest day ever!"

Annabelle ruffled Tommy's hair affectionately. "It was my pleasure Tommy. Always remember, a little sprinkle of kindness and a big scoop of love can brighten anyone's day."

Tommy returned to his village with a full belly and an even fuller heart. Inspired by Annabelle, he started his very own little ice cream cart. Even though his ice cream didn't have magical powers, Tommy made sure to add an extra helping of kindness, just like Annabelle taught him.

As Annabelle's fame grew, she stayed humble and focused on what mattered most - making people happy. And Annabelle and Tommy continued spreading smiles, one sweet scoop at a time. They knew the true power of ice cream was the way it brought people together and made the world feel like a friendlier place.

CHAPTER 3

Annabelle and Tommy became known throughout the land as the "Dynamic Duo of Delight". With their ice cream cart in tow, the two friends traveled near and far, serving up scoops of frozen happiness wherever they went.

One day, they met a little girl named Lily with puffy eyes and a quivering frown. "What's the matter?" Annabelle asked kindly, offering Lily a cone of her favorite flavor to cheer her up.

Sniffling, Lily replied, "I...I lost my teddy bear. His name is Bobo and he's my best friend in the whole world. Without him I feel so lonely."

Annabelle and Tommy looked at each other and nodded. They couldn't stand to see Lily so sad. "Cheer up Lily, we'll help you find Bobo. We promise!" Tommy said. "Annabelle and I make an un-BEAR-ably good team!"

Lily managed a tiny smile through her tears. With a new sense of hope, she joined her new friends on a quest to track down her missing bear. They searched high and low, asking everyone they met if they had seen Bobo. But as the sun began to set and the streets emptied, Lily started to lose heart.

Just as they were about to give up, Lily spotted a furry brown ear sticking out from behind a giant flowerpot. "Bobo!" she squealed, scooping up her beloved teddy and covering him in relieved hugs and kisses.

In that joyful moment, a idea struck Annabelle and Tommy like a lightning bolt made of rainbow sprinkles. Why stop at just selling ice cream? They could help find lost toys and treasures too!

They put their heads together and came up with a plan: The Magical Lost and Found. With Annabelle's ice cream magic and Tommy's clever detective skills, the Dynamic Duo would travel the land righting wrongs and reuniting sad children with their most cherished possessions.

Word of the Magical Lost and Found spread and soon Annabelle and Tommy had gathered a merry band of helpers. Children began calling them "The Rescuers of Happiness." No case was too big, no teddy bear too hidden for the Rescuers.

The Dynamic Duo and their team went wherever there were tears to dry and hearts to mend. And in helping others, they learned an important lesson: with kindness, determination and a little bit of magic, you can make the world brighter, one smile at a time.

Over the years, Annabelle, Tommy and the Rescuers shared countless adventures. And while finding lost toys was swell, the children taught them that the most precious treasures are the friendships you find and the happiness you create together.

CHAPTER 4

Thanks to the Rescuers of Happiness, the land became a kinder, more joyful place. The stories of their good deeds inspired more and more children to join in the fun. Pretty soon, it seemed like nearly every kid around wanted to make the world smile.

To celebrate all this newfound friendliness, Annabelle and Tommy dreamed up a big surprise: the first-ever Festival of Smiles! Children from all over were invited to come play games, make new pals, and of course, eat plenty of delicious ice cream.

When the big day arrived, the festival grounds looked like something out of a storybook. Colorful ribbons fluttered in the breeze, shiny balloons bobbed merrily, and the air smelled of sugar and sunshine. At the entrance, Annabelle and Tommy welcomed guests with cheek-splitting grins and great big bear hugs.

There were so many fun things to do! Kids could snuggle adorable teddy bears at the Cuddle Corner, follow clues to find hidden treasures on a Smile Scavenger Hunt, and even whisper their sweetest wishes into a magic wishing well. But the biggest hit of all was the Friendship Dance, where children from all over locked arms, spun in circles, and laughed until they were dizzy with delight.

As the sun started to dip in the sky and the fireflies came out to play, Annabelle and Tommy gathered everyone together. Standing on a big stage made of giant ice cream sandwich wafers, Annabelle said,

"Thank you all for coming to the Festival of Smiles! Today is about more than just yummy treats and fun games. It's about celebrating the magic that happens when we treat each other with kindness. Every single one of you has the power to make the world a little bit brighter, just by sharing a smile or lending a helping hand. So let's make a promise to always choose kindness, no matter what."

"We promise!" the children cheered, cross-crossing their hearts.

As the last round of ice cream was served and the final dance was danced, the Festival of Smiles came to a close. Tired but happy, the children hugged their new friends goodbye and headed home, carrying the warmth and joy of the day in their hearts.

From that day forward, the land was filled with more kindness and laughter than ever before. Though years passed and the children grew up, they never forgot the lessons they learned from Annabelle, Tommy, and the Rescuers of Happiness. They shared the stories of the Ice Cream Fairy with their own families, passing down the sweet secrets of kindness from generation to generation.

And so the legend of Annabelle and Tommy lived on, long after they hung up their aprons and retired their ice cream scoops. Theirs was a story of friendship, magic, and the power of a sweet, simple smile to change the world, one ice cream cone at a time.

THE END… Maybe

The Adventures of Annabelle

About The Book

Meet Annabelle, a curious girl with a heart as sweet as sugar, who discovers she has the power to make the most marvelous ice cream anyone has ever tasted. With her new friend Tommy by her side, Annabelle travels the land, serving up scoops of joy and kindness to everyone she meets.

But Annabelle and Tommy soon realize that their true calling is helping others. They form the Magical Lost and Found, a special team dedicated to reuniting sad children with their most treasured lost toys. With each teddy bear found and every smile restored Annabelle and Tommy learned that real magic comes from treating others with love and compassion.

Bursting with charming illustrations, giggle-worthy puns, and heartwarming lessons, this delightful chapter book reminds us that we all have the power to make the world a little sweeter. So, grab a spoon and dive into a story full of sprinkles, smiles, and the unbeatable power of friendship!

Perfect for young readers ages 6-10, "The Adventures of Annabelle" proves that anything is possible with a little bit of kindness and a whole lot of ice cream. Get ready to fall in love with Annabelle, Tommy, and their merry band of Rescuers in this enchanting, unforgettable tale.

Gus T Wynn